Let's Learn to Print

A Developmental Approach to Handwriting

Traditional Manuscript

by
Sherrill B. Flora

illustrated by
Janet Armbrust

Key Education
An imprint of Carson-Dellosa Publishing LLC
Greensboro, North Carolina

carsondellosa.com

Key Education
An imprint of Carson-Dellosa Publishing LLC
PO Box 35665
Greensboro, NC 27425 USA
carsondellosa.com

Credits
Author: Sherrill B. Flora
Illustrations: Janet Armbrust
Editors: Kelly Huxmann, George C. Flora
Cover Photography: © Comstock

ISBN 978-1-933052-00-7
06-079177784

Contents

Handwriting Ideas

Learning to print is an exciting experience for a young child. It is important that children learn how to print correctly. Here are some helpful hints that will assist children in learning how to print letters using the correct handwriting strokes.

SAND TRAYS

Take a cookie sheet and cover the bottom with either sand or salt. Have the children practice printing letters in the sand with their fingers. They will be able to feel how each letter is formed.

MOSAIC LETTERS

Gather fifty-two 4" x 6" index cards, glue, uncooked beans, macaroni, or seeds. Make 26 uppercase letters and 26 lower-case letters by drawing one letter on each card. Trace over the letters with glue and then lay the beans, pasta, or seeds on top of the glue. Let dry. When you have finished making the alphabet letters, they can be used for a variety of activities:

- Use as flash cards for letter identification.
- Place the cards in alphabetical order.
- Use the cards to match uppercase letters to lowercase letters.

CLAY OR PLAY DOUGH LETTERS

Prepare a set of alphabet cards ahead of time. Give the children play-dough or clay and teach them how to roll the clay so that it looks like a long worm. Have the children use the clay to form letters that correspond to the alphabet card.

When you first begin this activity, choose some of the easier alphabet letters such as O, C, V, X, L, and T. As the children become more skilled in shaping the letters, try introducing some of the more difficult letters.

GLUE LETTERS

Give each child a set of cards with one alphabet letter printed on each card. Let the children trace over the letters with white glue. Let the glue dry. Have the children use their index fingers to trace over the dried glue letters. This will allow them to feel how each letter is formed and to practice tracing the correct direction of each letter.

Review of Handwriting Strokes

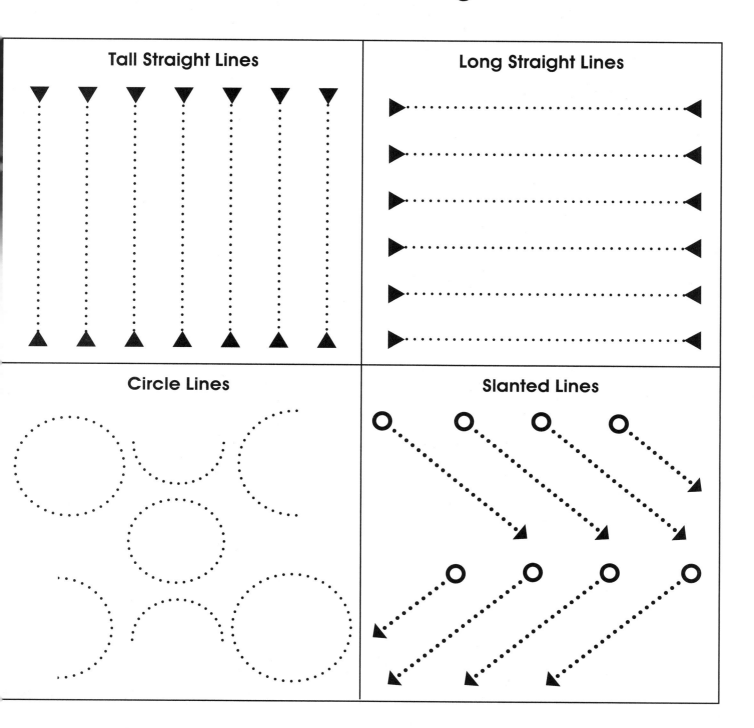

Tall Straight Lines

Long Straight Lines

Circle Lines

Slanted Lines

Name _____

Let's Learn About Guide Lines

This is → the top line.

This is → the middle line.

This is → the bottom line.

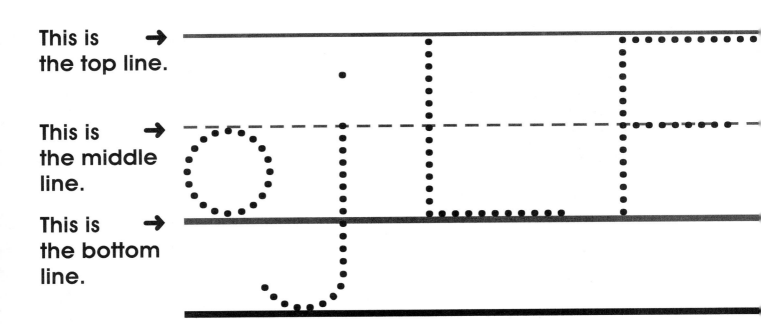

Try making some big letters. Be sure to touch the lines.

Name _____

- 6 -

Print your name.

Look at the laughing lion.

Color.

Trace the lowercase letters.

l l l .... lion

Print all by yourself. Circle your favorite letters.

Circle "I" and "L."

I l I T i L O I L Y l m L

Trace the uppercase letters.

L L L .... Look

Print all by yourself. Circle your favorite letters.

Circle your favorite letters.

Name _____

Trace and print.

1 ↓ **I** I I I I

Trace and print.

1 ↓ **L** L L L
2 →

Trace the sentence.

Leslie likes you.

Print the sentence all by yourself.

Trace the sentence.

Listen to her laugh.

Print the sentence all by yourself.

Print your name.

Ike said,"I like ice cream."

Color.

Trace the lowercase letters.

i i i i i i i i i i i i i i i ice

Print all by yourself.

Circle your favorite letters.

Circle "i" and "I."

h i I T i v I h J i r I

Trace the uppercase letters.

I I I I I I I I I I I I Ike

Print all by yourself.

Circle your favorite letters.

Let's Learn to Print: Traditional Manuscript

Circle your favorite letters.

Name

Trace and print.

i i i i i

Trace and print.

I I I I

Trace the sentence.

I like to print.

Print the sentence all by yourself.

Trace the sentence.

I like Mike and Ike.

Print the sentence all by yourself.

Print your name.

The tiger has a long tail. Color.

Trace the lowercase letters.

t t t t t t t t t t tent

Print all by yourself.

Circle your favorite letters.

Circle "T" and "t."

t L T t k h T P t I T t s

Trace the uppercase letters.

T T T T T T T T T Tm

Print all by yourself.

Circle your favorite letters.

Circle your favorite letters.

Name

Trace and print.

Trace and print.

Trace the sentence.

Tell Tom to listen.

Print the sentence all by yourself.

Trace the sentence.

Tigers have stripes.

Print the sentence all by yourself.

Aa Bb Cc Dd Ee Ff Gg Hh Ii Jj Kk Ll Mm Nn Oo Pp Qq Rr Ss Tt Uu Vv Ww Xx Yy Zz

Print your name.

The <u>ow</u>l <u>o</u>nly likes to read.
Color.

Trace the lowercase letters.

o o o o o o o o o off

Print all by yourself.   Circle your favorite letters.

Circle "O" and "o."

O o Q a O o S O K o m Q

Trace the uppercase letters.

O O O O O O O Owl

Print all by yourself.   Circle your favorite letters.

Circle your favorite letters.

Name

Trace and print.

Trace and print.

Trace the sentence.

Look at the books.

Print the sentence all by yourself.

Trace the sentence.

Look at Otto.

Print the sentence all by yourself.

C c

Print your name.

The cat likes cake and candy.

Color.

CANDY CORN

Carmels

CHOCOLATE COVERED CHERRIES

Trace the lowercase letters.

c c c c c c c c c c c cat

Print all by yourself.

Circle your favorite letters.

Circle "**C**" and "**c**."

c d e c C c O C o C e a

Trace the uppercase letters.

C C C C C C C C Car

Print all by yourself.

Circle your favorite letters.

Circle your favorite letters.

Name

Trace and print.

C C C C C

Trace and print.

C C C C

Trace the sentence.

Catch the ball, Cal!

Print the sentence all by yourself.

Trace the sentence.

Carol, come here!

Print the sentence all by yourself.

Print your name.

Ants love to eat apples.
Color.

Trace the lowercase letters.

a a a a a a a a ant

Print all by yourself.

Circle your favorite letters.

Circle "**A**" and "**a**."

A c a X V a V A X a A e

Trace the uppercase letters.

A A A A A A A A Ann

Print all by yourself.

Circle your favorite letters.

Circle your favorite letters.

Name

Trace and print.

a a a a a

Trace and print.

A A A A A

Trace the sentence.

Ann is very happy.

Print the sentence all by yourself.

Trace the sentence.

Apples are red.

Print the sentence all by yourself.

D d

Print your name.

Dave the dog likes to dig.

Color.

Trace the lowercase letters.

d d d d d d d d dog

Print all by yourself.

Circle your favorite letters.

Circle "**D**" and "**d**."

D d b h O D d D b d Q B

Trace the uppercase letters.

D D D D D D David

Print all by yourself.

Circle your favorite letters.

Circle your favorite letters.

Name _____

Trace and print.

d d d d d

Trace and print.

D D D D

Trace the sentence.

Did you draw that?

Print the sentence all by yourself.

Trace the sentence.

Ducks like to dive.

Print the sentence all by yourself.

Print your name.

Ellie Elephant is eating eggs.

Color.

Trace the lowercase letters.

e e e e e e e e egg

Print all by yourself.

Circle your favorite letters.

Circle "**E**" and "**e**."

e E F c E f e F a E e n

Trace the uppercase letters.

E E E E E E Ellie

Print all by yourself.

Circle your favorite letters.

Circle your favorite letters.

Name

Trace and print.

e   e   e   e   e

Trace and print.

E   E   E   E

Trace the sentence.

Eddie likes eggs.

Print the sentence all by yourself.

Trace the sentence.

Ellie eats beans.

Print the sentence all by yourself.

Print your name.

Fred the fox is fishing.
Color.

Trace the lowercase letters.

f f f f f f f f f f f fish

Print all by yourself.   Circle your favorite letters.

Circle "**F**" and "**f**."

F f j f E e H F h F M f

Trace the uppercase letters.

F F F F F F F F Frank

Print all by yourself.   Circle your favorite letters.

Circle your favorite letters.

Name _____

Trace and print.

f f f f

Trace and print.

F F F F

Trace the sentence.

Find the funny face.

Print the sentence all by yourself.

Trace the sentence.

Fred is a fluffy fox.

Print the sentence all by yourself.

Print your name.

Hilda Hippo has a hat.

Color.

Trace the lowercase letters.

h h h h h h h h h h h h h hat

Print all by yourself.

Circle your favorite letters.

Circle "**H**" and "**h**."

h n H b k H H h K h n H d

Trace the uppercase letters.

H H H H H H H H H H H H Harry

Print all by yourself.

Circle your favorite letters.

Circle your favorite letters.

Name

Trace and print.

h h h h h

Trace and print.

H H H H

Trace the sentence.

Hike up the hill.

Print the sentence all by yourself.

Trace the sentence.

Harriet is a hen.

Print the sentence all by yourself.

G g

Print your name.

The goats are giving gifts. Color.

Trace the lowercase letters.

g g g g g g g g goat

Print all by yourself.   Circle your favorite letters.

Circle "**G**" and "**g**."

q g p g G Q P G C G g

Trace the uppercase letters.

G G G G G G G G

Print all by yourself.   Circle your favorite letters.

Circle your favorite letters.

Name

Trace and print.

g g g g g

Trace and print.

G G G G

Trace the sentence.

Girls like to giggle.

Print the sentence all by yourself.

Trace the sentence.

Gus has a goat.

Print the sentence all by yourself.

Print your name.

Joe Jaguar jumps rope.
Color.

Trace the lowercase letters.

j j j j j j j j j j j jump

Print all by yourself.

Circle your favorite letters.

Circle "J" and "j."

J P q n j J J g j h J U j

Trace the uppercase letters.

J J J J J J J J John

Print all by yourself.

Circle your favorite letters.

Circle your favorite letters.

Name

Trace and print.

j j j j j

Trace and print.

J J J J J

Trace the sentence.

Jack and Jill jump.

Print the sentence all by yourself.

Trace the sentence.

John flies a jet.

Print the sentence all by yourself.

Print your name.

The queen makes quilts.

Color.

Trace the lowercase letters.

q q q q q q q quiet

Print all by yourself.

Circle your favorite letters.

Circle "**Q**" and "**q**."

q c p q Q O O q C Q a Q D

Trace the uppercase letters.

Q Q Q Q Q Q Queen

Print all by yourself.

Circle your favorite letters.

Circle your favorite letters.

Name

Trace and print.

q q q q q

Trace and print.

Q Q Q Q

Trace the sentence.

Quack like a duck.

Print the sentence all by yourself.

Trace the sentence.

The queen quilts.

Print the sentence all by yourself.

Print your name.

Peggy Pig plans to be a pilot.
Color.

Trace the lowercase letters.

p p p p p p p p p p p pig

Print all by yourself.   Circle your favorite letters.

Circle "**P**" and "**p**."

p q g P d p P B J p b P

Trace the uppercase letters.

P P P P P P P P P Pink

Print all by yourself.   Circle your favorite letters.

Circle your favorite letters.

Name _____

Trace and print.

P P P P P

Trace and print.

P P P P P

Trace the sentence.

Pablo has a pet pig.

Print the sentence all by yourself.

_____

_____

Trace the sentence.

Pandas are pretty.

Print the sentence all by yourself.

_____

_____

Print your name.

The <u>u</u>nicorn has an <u>u</u>mbrella.

Color.

Trace the lowercase letters.

u u u u u u u u u under

Print all by yourself.

Circle your favorite letters.

Circle "**U**" and "**u**."

N u U h U D u U b u n V

Trace the uppercase letters.

U U U U U U U U U Up

Print all by yourself.

Circle your favorite letters.

Circle your favorite letters.

Name

Trace and print.

u u u u

Trace and print.

U U U U

Trace the sentence.

Use your umbrella.

Print the sentence all by yourself.

Trace the sentence.

Unicorns are cute.

Print the sentence all by yourself.

S s

Print your name.

Sara Seal sits in the sun.

Color.

Trace the lowercase letters.

s s s s s s s s s s sit

Print all by yourself.

Circle your favorite letters.

Circle "**S**" and "**s**."

X S s C S e K S u s E s

Trace the uppercase letters.

S S S S S S S S Sam

Print all by yourself.

Circle your favorite letters.

Let's Learn to Print: Traditional Manuscript

Circle your favorite letters.

Name _____

Trace and print.

s s s s s

Trace and print.

S S S S

Trace the sentence.

Sue sings songs.

Print the sentence all by yourself.

Trace the sentence.

Seals slip and slide.

Print the sentence all by yourself.

Print your name.

Baby Bear blows bubbles.

Color.

Trace the lowercase letters.

b b b b b b b b ball

Print all by yourself.

Circle your favorite letters.

Circle "**B**" and "**b**."

b d p B D B d b B d P b

Trace the uppercase letters.

B B B B B B B B Ben

Print all by yourself.

Circle your favorite letters.

Circle your favorite letters.

Name

Trace and print.

b b b b b

Trace and print.

B B B B

Trace the sentence.

Bob likes baseball.

Print the sentence all by yourself.

Trace the sentence.

Give baby a bottle.

Print the sentence all by yourself.

Print your name.

Robert Rabbit runs the race.

Color.

Trace the lowercase letters.

r   r   r   r   r   r   r   r   r   r   r   r   run

Print all by yourself.   Circle your favorite letters.

Circle "**R**" and "**r**."

r   P   R   r   n   u   R   B   h   R   H   r

Trace the uppercase letters.

R   R   R   R   R   R   R   R   R   R   Rob

Print all by yourself.   Circle your favorite letters.

Circle your favorite letters.

Name

Trace and print.

r r r r r

Trace and print.

R R R R

Trace the sentence.

Ride in the rocket.

Print the sentence all by yourself.

Trace the sentence.

Rock and roll!

Print the sentence all by yourself.

Ned Newt reads the newspaper.

Print your name.

Color.

Trace the lowercase letters.

n n n n n n n n n n nest

Print all by yourself.

Circle your favorite letters.

Circle "**N**" and "**n**."

n N M n b n N V M m h N

Trace the uppercase letters.

N N N N N N N N Nick

Print all by yourself.

Circle your favorite letters.

Circle your favorite letters.

Name

Trace and print.

n n n n n

Trace and print.

N N N N N

Trace the sentence.

Ned is so nice.

Print the sentence all by yourself.

Trace the sentence.

Nan is never late.

Print the sentence all by yourself.

Trace the lowercase letters.

Print your name.

Many monkeys make music.

Color.

m m m m m m m m m m mine

Print all by yourself.

Circle your favorite letters.

Circle "**M**" and "**m**."

m N m H M u M w M W m w

Trace the uppercase letters.

M M M M M M M Mike

Print all by yourself.

Circle your favorite letters.

Circle your favorite letters.

Name

Trace and print.

m m m m m

Trace and print.

M M M M

Trace the sentence.

Man on the moon.

Print the sentence all by yourself.

Trace the sentence.

Martin is a mouse.

Print the sentence all by yourself.

Print your name.

Violet Vulture plays the violin.

Color.

Trace the lowercase letters.

V V v v v v v v v v vase

Print all by yourself.   Circle your favorite letters.

Circle "**V**" and "**v**."

v V x V U w v W N V x v

Trace the uppercase letters.

V V V V V V V V V Vern

Print all by yourself.   Circle your favorite letters.

Aa Bb Cc Dd Ee Ff Gg Hh Ii Jj Kk Ll Mm Nn Oo Pp Qq Rr Ss Tt Uu Vv Ww Xx Yy Zz

Circle your favorite letters.

Name

Trace and print.

V v v v v

Trace and print.

V V V V

Trace the sentence.

Violets are lovely.

Print the sentence all by yourself.

Trace the sentence.

Vultures are very big.

Print the sentence all by yourself.

Print your name.

Color.

Yani Yak loves his yellow yo-yo.

Trace the lowercase letters.

y y y y y y y y y y yoke

Print all by yourself.

Circle your favorite letters.

Circle "**Y**" and "**y**."

y x y g V Y j W y X Y w Y

Trace the uppercase letters.

Y Y Y Y Y Y Y Y Yak

Print all by yourself.

Circle your favorite letters.

Circle your favorite letters.

Name

Trace and print.

y y y y y

Trace and print.

Y Y Y Y

Trace the sentence.

The yak is yawning.

Print the sentence all by yourself.

Trace the sentence.

Yogurt is yummy!

Print the sentence all by yourself.

Print your name.

Wally Walrus swims in the water.
Color.

Trace the lowercase letters.

w w w w w w water

Print all by yourself.

Circle your favorite letters.

Circle "**W**" and "**w**."

w m w v W U V w W X W m

Trace the uppercase letters.

W W W W W W Wow

Print all by yourself.

Circle your favorite letters.

Circle your favorite letters.

Name

Trace and print.

w   w   w   w

Trace and print.

W   W   W   W

Trace the sentence.

Wash the windows.

Print the sentence all by yourself.

Trace the sentence.

Worms wiggle!

Print the sentence all by yourself.

Print your name.

<u>X</u>avier plays the <u>x</u>ylophone.

Color.

Trace the lowercase letters.

X X x x x x x x x box

Print all by yourself.

Circle your favorite letters.

Circle "**X**" and "**x**."

x y v X W v V X x Y x X

Trace the uppercase letters.

X X X X X X X X-ray

Print all by yourself.

Circle your favorite letters.

Circle your favorite letters.

Name _____

Trace and print.

X x x x x

Trace and print.

X X X X

Trace the sentence.

X-ray the box.

Print the sentence all by yourself.

Trace the sentence.

The fox is furry.

Print the sentence all by yourself.

K k

Kelly Kangaroo flies a kite.

Color.

Print your name.

Trace the lowercase letters.

k k k k k k k k k kite

Print all by yourself.

Circle your favorite letters.

Circle "**K**" and "**k**."

K k X v W K Y k T E k K

Trace the uppercase letters.

K K K K K K K Katie

Print all by yourself.

Circle your favorite letters.

Circle your favorite letters.

Name

Trace and print.

k k k k k

Trace and print.

K K K K

Trace the sentence.

The koala is kooky.

Print the sentence all by yourself.

Trace the sentence.

Keshia is very kind.

Print the sentence all by yourself.

Print your name.

Zack Zebra zips his zipper.

Color.

Trace the lowercase letters.

z z z z z z z z z zoo

Print all by yourself.

Circle your favorite letters.

Circle "Z" and "z."

T z A Z z Z v L Z S s z

Trace the uppercase letters.

Z Z Z Z Z Z Z Z Z Zelda

Print all by yourself.

Circle your favorite letters.

Circle your favorite letters.

Name

Trace and print.

Z z z z z

Trace and print.

Z Z Z Z Z

Trace the sentence.

Zebras have stripes.

Print the sentence all by yourself.

Trace the sentence.

Ziggy ran zigzag.

Print the sentence all by yourself.

Review
Lowercase Letters

Print your name.

Trace.

a b c d e f g h

i j k l m n o p q

r s t u v w x y z

Print your own lowercase alphabet.

Review
Uppercase Letters

Print your name.

Trace.

A B C D E F G H I

J K L M N O P Q R

S T U V W X Y Z

Print your own uppercase alphabet.

FINAL ASSESSMENT

Print your name.

Print your own lowercase alphabet.

Print your own uppercase alphabet.

Aa Bb Cc Dd Ee Ff Gg Hh Ii Jj Kk Ll Mm Nn Oo Pp Qq Rr Ss Tt Uu Vv Ww Xx Yy Zz

KE-804006 © Carson-Dellosa

Let's Learn to Print: Traditional Manuscript

Standards Correlations for Let's Learn to Print
A Developmental Approach to Handwriting (Traditional Manuscript)

This book supports the NCTE/IRA Standards for the English Language Arts and the recommended teaching practices outlined in the NAEYC/IRA position statement Learning to Read and Write: Developmentally Appropriate Practices for Young Children.

NCTE/IRA Standards for the English Language Arts

Each activity in this book supports one or more of the following standards:

1. **Students read many different types of print and nonprint texts for a variety of purposes.** Students read directions in order to complete the activities in this book.

2. **Students use a variety of strategies to build meaning while reading.** The activities in this book promote letter recognition skills essential to effective reading.

3. **Students communicate in spoken, written, and visual form for a variety of purposes and a variety of audiences.** In *Let's Learn to Print*, students communicate in written form, writing letters and words, to illustrate their progress in learning to write.

NAEYC/IRA Position Statement Learning to Read and Write: Developmentally Appropriate Practices for Young Children

Each activity in this book supports one or more of the following recommended teaching practices for kindergarten and primary students:

1. **Teachers provide opportunities for students to write many different kinds of texts for different purposes.** *Let's Learn to Print* includes opportunities for students to practice printing letters and words in order to improve their handwriting skills.

2. **Teachers provide writing experiences that allow children to develop from the use of nonconventional writing forms to the use of more conventional forms.** In *Let's Learn to Print*, students practice proper letter formation, which allows them to move toward conventional penmanship.